Mason Jar

Quick and Easy Recipes for Lunches on the Go, in a Jar

Table of Contents

INTRODUCTION 1

CHICKEN LUNCH RECIPES IN A MASON JAR 3

    Chicken Cordon bleu in a Jar 5
    Mexican Chicken in a Jar 7
    Pesto Chicken in a jar 9

BEEF LUNCH RECIPES IN A MASON JAR 11

    Beef Tacos in a jar 13
    Chili with Cornbread topping 15
    Macaroni with mini Meatballs in a Jar 17

PORK LUNCH RECIPES IN A MASON JAR 19

    Pulled Pork Parfait 21
    Spicy Pork Chili 23
    Sparerib Salad in a Jar 25

SEAFOOD LUNCH RECIPES IN A MASON JAR 27

    Cajun grilled Shrimp in a jar 29
    Salmon Nicoise in a Mason jar 31
    Deconstructed Tuna Sushi in a jar 33

VEGETARIAN LUNCH RECIPES IN A MASON JAR 35

    Spring Style Sprout salad 37
    Healthy Burrito in a jar 39
    Penne pesto in a jar 41
    Quinoa Salad 43
    Asian Salad in a Jar 45

CONCLUSION 47

Your Free Bonus: Get this FREE Recipe Book

As a thank you, I want to give you this amazing collection of **101 Quick and Easy Recipes**, completely free of charge, as my gift to you. Download it now!

Click here to get it FREE!!

http://bit.ly/free101recipes

Introduction

I want to thank you and congratulate you for downloading the book, *"Mason Jar Lunches"*.

This book contains proven steps and strategies on how to make lunches on the go in Mason jars.

Imagine having your lunch already prepared and in the fridge for you before you go to work. Imagine having your lunch stay fresh in the fridge all week. Well, the real trick is making your lunch in a mason jar. The jar keeps food fresher for longer than Tupper-wear, it's microwavable, is air tight and keeps ingredients separate so that, as long as you layer it correctly, everything stays perfect all day. And the best part is that your lunch looks adorable in a jar, all your co-workers will be jealous.

This book is filled with recipes of Mason jar lunches that are healthy and easy to make. Anyone with basic knowledge of cooking will be able to make and prepare these meals. Please enjoy what I will have in store for you and enjoy these lunches in Mason jars which are all proven to be delicious and original. I promise you won't break a sweat making these recipes as these are super easy, but extremely tasty.

Have fun and experiment with the ingredients, mix and match these recipes if you like as I had fun making these meals as well as writing and sharing them with you too.

Thanks again for downloading this book, I hope you enjoy it!

Chicken Lunch Recipes in a Mason Jar

Chicken is the protein of choice for everybody as it is affordable and available anywhere. This protein is one of the most versatile ingredients out there as it can be grilled, fried, poached, steamed and even stewed. Chicken has great flavor and an ingredient associated with health conscious people. As you know chicken is high in protein and low in fat that is if you remove the skin and use only the white meat which is the chicken breast. So enjoy these chicken recipes which I have made for you and have your family and friends look in awe when they see how delicious your lunch can be.

Chicken Cordon bleu in a Jar

Ingredients

6 pieces chicken breast, deboned

Salt and pepper to taste

6 slices of smoked ham, country ham or any other ham you like

6 slices of cheese, Swiss is preferred but mozzarella would be great too

½ cup unsalted butter, melted

3 teaspoons parsley, chopped

1 cup coarse bread crumbs

Directions

Lay your chicken breasts in a flat surface while covering each piece with a plastic wrap. With a meat tenderizer, pound your chicken breasts so that they will become flat and wide then season with salt and pepper to taste. Top each chicken piece with a slice of ham and a slice of cheese.

Roll each chicken breast so that the ham and cheese are enclosed in the chicken roll. Place each roll vertically into a greased Mason jar. In a small mixing bowl mix together your butter, parsley and coarse breadcrumbs then top each chicken in a Mason jar with your breadcrumbs. Once these are done, place your jar in a sheet pan and bake for 45 minutes in a 350 degree oven till cooked. Once done you may eat right away or place in the refrigerator when it has cooled as it can stay for a week or so. To reheat you may place in the microwave for 3-5 minutes or in the oven.

Mexican Chicken in a Jar

Ingredients

4 tablespoons fresh salsa or bottled

1 chicken breast, grilled seasoned with taco seasoning

4 tablespoons cilantro, chopped

4 tablespoons whole corn kernels, drained

4 tablespoons cheddar cheese, shredded or as much as you want

2 large bell peppers, roasted and sliced

1 avocado, deseeded and diced

½ cup crushed tortilla chips

Directions

Layer your ingredients in the Mason jar with the salsa going in first. Top with your chicken so that it can marinate and absorb the flavors of the salsa. Next is to add in your cilantro, whole corn kernels and cheddar cheese.

Arrange your avocado and bell peppers on top then sprinkle your crushed tortilla chips on top.

Serve right away or you may chill for up to 3 days. Enjoy this Mexican inspired chicken dish.

Pesto Chicken in a jar

Ingredients

1 chicken breast, deboned and cut into chunks

3 tablespoons extra virgin olive oil

1 medium tomato, diced

1 medium red onion, chopped

1 large bell pepper, roasted and sliced

½ cup fresh mozzarella, torn into pieces

4 slices of pepperoni

½ cup spinach, rinsed

Directions

Marinate your chicken in some store bought or homemade pesto for at least an hour then grill or pan fry till cooked and set aside.

Arrange your Mason jar meal by pouring in your olive oil first in the bottom followed by your tomatoes and red onions and then topped with your roasted bell peppers.

Add in your fresh mozzarella and your cooked chicken bits. Finish off with the chopped pepperoni slices and some spinach to cover.

Keep refrigerated for up to 5 days until needed. This may not be heated when eaten as this is a great dish eaten cold.

Beef Lunch Recipes in a Mason Jar

Who doesn't love beef, or steak for that matter? Everybody does and it is even easy to buy, just ask your' most trusted butcher to give you their best cut of the day or what he recommends for your planned meal. Lean beef is one of the most sought after meat for high protein content. It is also very healthy and usually tastes much better the day after when cooked in stews or braised. Imagine having a steak or beef stew for lunch, in a jar! That would be really great and convenient. Beef is a great ingredient for satisfying ones hunger as it can make you feel full and happy every time you eat it. So enjoy these beef recipes and cook them with love as you may feel its warmth when you eat it.

Beef Tacos in a jar

Ingredients

3 tablespoons salsa, homemade or store bought

1 large tomato, diced

1 medium red onion, chopped

½ piece plantain, sliced

½ piece avocado, deseeded and diced

200 grams ground beef

1 tablespoon taco seasoning

Salt and pepper to taste

Spinach

Directions

In a medium size mixing bowl, add in your ground beef mixed with taco seasoning and seasoned with salt and pepper. Pan fry this ground beef mixture until fully cooked and set aside.

Layer your Mason jar with the salsa in first at the bottom then followed by your tomatoes and red onions. After these two have been placed it will be time now to add the plantains and the avocado.

Add in your seasoned ground beef and top with your spinach leaves and enjoy.

Store in the chiller for 3 – 5 days or until needed. This is a great way to experience and enjoy a Mexican meal in a jar.

Chili with Cornbread topping

Ingredients

1 onion, chopped

3 cloves garlic, chopped

500 grams ground beef

Salt and pepper to taste

1 can tomato sauce

1 can black or red beans, rinsed and drained

1 can re-fried beans

Chili powder and cayenne pepper to taste

1/2 teaspoon Onion powder

1/2 teaspoon Garlic powder

1/2 teaspoon Cumin

Brown sugar to taste

1 package cornbread batter, store bought

Directions

In a large pot, saute your onions and garlic in oil then add in your ground beef, season with salt and pepper and cook while breaking up the beef until no more pink parts are seen.

Add in your tomato sauce, refried beans and black beans then season with chili powder, cayenne pepper, onion powder, garlic powder and cumin. Simmer for 10 minutes and season to taste. Once cooked, ladle in your chili inside the Mason jars around a little over half full then top with your mixed cornbread batter.

Bake in a 375 degree oven for 20 minutes until the cornbread is cooked and when a toothpick inserted is comes out clean.

Let your chili cool and refrigerate till needed. To serve just heat in the microwave for 5 -7 minutes.

Macaroni with mini Meatballs in a Jar

Ingredients

1 medium onion chopped finely

3 teaspoons olive oil

2 cloves garlic, chopped

1 liter beef stock

250 grams ground beef

Salt and pepper to taste

1 egg

½ cup fine breadcrumbs

2 teaspoons onion powder

1 teaspoon garlic powder

1/2 cup Parmesan cheese, grated

1 can diced tomatoes

250 grams macaroni, cooked

3 teaspoons butter

Salt and pepper to taste

Directions

Saute the onions in olive oil using a large pot while continuously stirring. Add in your garlic and the stock then Bring to a boil. In a medium sized mixing bowl mix in your ground beef, egg, bread crumbs, salt and pepper to taste, onions, garlic powder and parmesan cheese until well blended. Form this mixture into small balls and one by one drop them into the boiling stock to boil for 5 minutes.

Add in your tomatoes, macaroni, butter, cheese and salt and pepper to taste while stirring frequently until pasta is al dente. Pour into your Mason jars and eat right away. If you want to store them just let it cool and cover then refrigerate as these can last for up to 4 days. To reheat just microwave for around 5 minutes till heated through.

Pork Lunch Recipes in a Mason Jar

Pork, one of the best proteins to cook, not for its health content as these are really high in fat but most sought after for its flavor and versatility too. Pork can be paired with almost anything and may be cooked any way you want. If you have noticed, a lot of the most popular and flavorful foods around are generally pork such as back-ribs, pulled pork, roast pork loin and bacon. These dishes are the result of the complementing power of pork and imagine having these as your lunch in mason jars, it could be really convenient and very satisfying. Our tummies would be very happy with such a treat and will be very full afterwards. So enjoy these really yummy pork recipes in Mason jars that will surely have you wanting more.

Pulled Pork Parfait

Ingredients

1 cup pulled pork, leftover from yesterday or freshly made batch

½ cup mashed potatoes, either store bought or homemade

1 can refried beans

1 Mason Jar

Directions

In a saucepan, heat your refried beans until heated through then place in the bottom of the Mason jar.

Top this with your heated mashed potatoes and finish with the pulled pork on top.

Add in some more BBQ sauce if you like and also some hot sauce for some heat. Enjoy right away or place in the refrigerator for up to two days and just microwave for 3 minutes to serve.

Spicy Pork Chili

Ingredients

1 large onion, dicced

1 large bell pepper, diced

2 garlic cloves, chopped

1 jalapeño, chopped

500 grams, ground pork

1 large can whole peeled tomatoes

1 can chickpeas, drained

1 can red beans, drained

1 can kidney beans, drained

½ cup parsley, chopped

Olive oil

Salt and pepper to taste

3 teaspoons chili powder

1/2 teaspoon garlic powder

½ teaspoon cumin

½ teaspoon cayenne

Directions

Saute your onions and garlic in a large pot with olive oil then add in your pork. Cook for 10 minutes and add the jalapeno and the bell peppers for another 5 minutes.

Add in all remaining ingredients plus a cup of water then bring to a boil and simmer while covered for an hour. Season to taste with salt and pepper as well as other spices you like.

Place in your mason jars and eat right away or refrigerate for up to 5 days till needed. Enjoy!

Sparerib Salad in a Jar

Ingredients

3 tablespoons ranch dressing, store bought

½ carrot, sliced

5 cherry tomatoes, halved

5 strawberries, halved

¼ cup blueberries

150 Pork spareribs, marinated in steak sauce and grill

½ cup romaine salad chopped

¼ cup swiss cheese grated or shredded cheddar cheese

Directions

Take your Mason jar and place your first layer of dressing in the bottom of the jar. Top with your carrots and tomatoes.

Add in your strawberries and blueberries and arrange each layer nicely to protect your other ingredients from the dressing.

Place your steak on top followed by the chopped lettuce. Finish everything off with your swiss cheese or grated cheddar cheese. Eat right away or refrigerate till needed.

Enjoy this very healthy and hearty steak salad with mixed berries.

Seafood Lunch Recipes in a Mason Jar

After you've had that pork overload, now it's time to go a step down to seafood and have a rewarding seafood meal which is low in fat, has moderately enough protein and really high omega 3. The possibilities for seafood are endless as there a really wide range of seafood that we can have, the only problem is you won't be able to fit the entire ocean in your Mason jar. But we can at least try with some very flavorful and common seafood ingredients and preparations. In this seafood part of my recipe book I will be making you some very healthy and easy recipes which you can make for you and your family for let's say Seafood Saturday or Sunday, Enjoy!

Cajun grilled Shrimp in a jar

Ingredients

1 large bell pepper, sliced

1 large onion, sliced

5 medium sized shrimp, peeled and deveined

3 tablespoons guacamole, store bought or made fresh

½ cup spinach, rinsed and patted dry

Directions

Saute your bell peppers in olive oil and season to taste with salt, pepper and Cajun seasoning and set aside.

Saute your onions in olive oil and season with salt and pepper and set aside.

Season your shrimp with olive oil, lemon juice, salt, pepper and Cajun seasoning then grill till cooked

Layer your ingredients in a Mason jar with the sautéed bell peppers first followed by your sautéed onions.

Top the mixture with your grilled Cajun shrimp and spoon in your guacamole on top.

Finish off with your spinach leaves and eat right away or refrigerate for up to 4 days. When ready to eat just take out of the jar onto a plate or eat as is with a fork, enjoy!

Salmon Nicoise in a Mason jar

Ingredients

3 tablespoons vinaigrette of your choice, preferably citrus vinaigrette

7 green beans, sliced into 3 each

1 hard-boiled egg, diced

5 cherry tomatoes, halved

¼ cup black olives, sliced

2 medium potatoes, boiled and diced

150 grams salmon, grilled or pan fried

Directions

For your first layer, place in the vinaigrette of your choice in the bottom of your Mason jar followed by your blanched green beans.

Top with your diced hard-boiled egg and cherry tomatoes. Add in your sliced black olives and also your potatoes. Make sure to arrange them nicely.

For the last layer top your salmon, you may slice into chunks or you may place it whole whichever you may prefer then serve. If you want to keep it just refrigerate as it will stay for 5 days and just take out and toss everything to eat.

Deconstructed Tuna Sushi in a jar

Ingredients

½ cup cooked white or sushi rice

3 teaspoons rice wine vinegar

1 ½ teaspoon sugar

1 ½ teaspoon soy sauce

1 sheet nori, cut into smaller pieces

4 tablespoons carrot, shredded

¼ cucumber sliced julienne

½ piece avocado, deseeded and diced

2 tablespoons lime juice

Pickled ginger

Wasabi paste

Directions

Dissolve your sugar in vinegar and mix in your rice with the soy sauce, mix well to combine.

Layer your ingredients in a Mason jar with the nori first in the bottom and then followed by a third of the rice. Add in your shredded carrots and another third of the rice.

Place your pickled ginger with the avocado slices you have and top with the rice that you have left.

Lastly place your cucumber and topped with your nori and a splash of your lime juice to finish.

Serve right away or chill for up to two days only as your rice may spoil if left for long. Enjoy these Japanese inspired mason Jar meal from the comfort of your home or office.

Vegetarian Lunch Recipes in a Mason Jar

Vegetables are really great for you and with these vegetarian Mason jar recipes, nothing can be more convenient than having these with you for lunch. You may still have the protein you need from some nuts and also have all the fiber that you want from a very wide range of vegetables available in the market. If you want to heighten these recipes to another level, just choose all organic vegetables as these are all free of chemicals and naturally grown. So what are you waiting for plant a vegetable garden or just buy from the market for now but still enjoy these healthy and low calorie vegetarian recipes made by me for you in Mason jars.

Spring Style Sprout salad

Ingredients

1 can garbanzos, drained

1 small carrot, grated

7 cherry tomatoes, halved

1 cup edamame beans, shelled

¼ cup pine nuts or any type of nut you like

1 cup of fresh sprouts of any kind or you can mix it up such as bean sprouts, alfalfa sprouts or mustard sprouts

For the basil vinaigrette:

¼ cup extra virgin olive oil

3 tablespoons red wine vinegar

½ cup basil leaves, chopped

1 teaspoon whole grain mustard

Salt and pepper to taste

Directions

Make first the vinaigrette in a medium bowl by adding your extra virgin olive oil, red wine vinegar, basil leaves, whole grain mustard and season to taste with salt and pepper then place in the bottom of your Mason jar as the first layer.

Place the garbanzos next in the jar and follow it with the other hard vegetables such as carrots, tomatoes, edamame beans and your nuts of choice.

Lastly top with your choice or mix of sprouts then eat right away or refrigerate for up to 5 days. When ready to eat just shake your jar very well and pour on a plate or bowl to eat.

Healthy Burrito in a jar

Ingredients

1 cup quinoa, cooked according to packets directions

1 cup canned black beans, drained

3 cups lettuce, rinsed and chopped

1 cup kale leaves, chopped

½ cup greek yoghurt or light yoghurt

2 cups of assorted sprouts of your choice

1 cup tomato salsa, homemade or store bought

Directions

Place your cooked quinoa as the first layer of your meal in the mason jar. Add the black beans which you have drained followed by your chopped lettuce and chopped kale. Top with your cherry tomato salsa and your assorted sprouts then a scoop of the yoghurt.

With this recipe you have to eat it right away as you can see the dressing is on top however if you want to make this recipe and keep it for a couple of days, just rearrange the layers by placing the salsa and yoghurt first and then your black beans followed by quinoa, chopped kale and lettuce and finished with the sprouts. Chill for up to 3 day or until needed.

Penne pesto in a jar

Ingredients

1 cup penne pasta, cooked al dente

¼ cup of your pasta water or tap water

2 garlic cloves

1 cup basil, fresh and rinsed

4 tablespoons walnuts, toasted

4 tablespoons extra virgin olive oil

Salt and pepper to taste

½ cup parmesan cheese

5 cherry tomatoes, halved

¼ cup fresh mozzarella cheese or feta cheese crumbled

Directions

Make your pesto first by taking a food processor and adding in your basil, olive oil, walnuts, garlic olive oil and little of the pasta water to moisten the pesto. Season with salt and pepper and place in the bottom of your mason jar.

Next step is to add in your halved cherry tomatoes and a layer of your choice of cheese, it really depends what you like. Lastly the cooked penne pasta and what you have to do now is just give this jar a shake and you have pasta on the go. Just chill if you want it for a later time and then just mix and microwave for 3 minutes to serve. Enjoy!

Quinoa Salad

Ingredients

1 cup quinoa, cooked according to packet's directions

6 cherry tomatoes, washed and halved

1 cucumber, deseeded, peeled and diced into cubes

½ cup parsley, washed and chopped

1 can chickpeas, drained

3 tablespoons dressing of your choice

Salt and pepper to taste

Directions

Arrange your dressing first as the first layer of your Mason jar. Top these with the halved cherry tomatoes and arrange well so that the dressing can't reach the top.

Add in your cucumbers and chickpeas as the next layer. Top with your cooked quinoa and parsley leaves then season with some salt and pepper to taste.

To serve just shake the bottle and pour in a plate or you may still shake and eat straight from the jar.

If not to be eaten right away, just place in the chiller for up to 3 days until needed.

Asian Salad in a Jar

Ingredients

½ cup Edamame, shelled

½ cup Cubed Cucumbers, peeled and deseeded

1 large Tomato, diced

¼ cup Snap Peas

1 Mandarin Orange, sliced into segments

1 small carrot, shredded

½ cup Sprouts, any kind you like

Lettuce or some baby spinach

Asian dressing of your choice may it be mayo based or vinaigrette

Directions

Place your Asian dressing the mason jar first to make the first layer then top with your tomatoes and cucumbers.

Then your edamame and snap peas next followed by the mandarin orange and carrots. Finish off with your sprouts and choice of greens.

Give the jar a shake and pour in a plate or eat directly on a plate. If chilled it may keep for up to 4 days. Enjoy!

Conclusion

Thank you again for downloading this book!

I hope this book was able to help you to in making Lunches on the go using Mason jars.

The next step is to enjoy and start cooking these recipes whether you like chicken, pork, beef, seafood or vegetarian recipes everything is in there. My suggestion, try cooking and making all of them have some variations every day. Cook a whole batch every weekend of each protein or vegetable so that you may have a different meal every day. Make variations and have the chicken substituted with the pork if you like or even have a beef dish changed with tofu to make it vegetarian. Check out what recipe components you like as this is a very versatile recipe book where you will be able to mix and match any ingredient of your liking. Enjoy and have a great Mason jar cook-off and see how healthy these meals can be as these can give you a whole lot of savings and time for your family. Also try packing these for your kid's lunches and snacks as they will appreciate how cool this can be with all the flavors that only restaurants can make but now in your lunchboxes.

Finally, if you enjoyed this book, then I'd like to ask you for a favor, would you be kind enough to leave a review for this book on Amazon? It'd be greatly appreciated!

<u>Click here to leave a review for this book on Amazon!</u>

http://amzn.to/13WVU1U

Thank you and good luck!

Check Out My Other Books

Below you'll find some of my other popular books that are popular on Amazon and Kindle as well. Simply click on the links below to check them out.

[Mason Jar Meals: Quick and Easy Recipes for Meals on the Go, in a Jar](#)

[Mason Jar Salads: Quick and Easy Recipes for Salads on the Go, in a Jar](#)

[Make Ahead Freezer Meals: Because wouldn't it be nice if dinner was already in the freezer?](#)

[Canning and Preserving: Everything You Need to Know About How to Can and Preserve Anything!](#)

[DIY Household Hacks: Astonishingly simple but clever tips, tricks and shortcuts that will make cleaning and organizing your house easier than you can possibly imagine](#)

Slow Cooker Cookbook: Creative and delicious recipes for things you never knew you could make in a slow cooker

If the links do not work, for whatever reason, you can simply search for these titles on the Amazon website to find them.

Don't Forget Your Free Bonus: Get this FREE Recipe Book

Do you waste your money on take-out because you don't have time to cook? Do you want more variety in your diet? Well this Recipe Book is for you!!!

"101 Quick & Easy Recipes" is the quickest and easiest way to create gourmet and great tasting meals all in 30 minutes or less! Inside this magnificent book, you'll get **101 Recipes** you'll absolutely love, all of which can be made quickly and easily... in 30 minutes or less!!

As a thank you, I want to give you this amazing collection of recipes, completely free of charge, as my gift to you. There is no catch... it's really free, I promise. Just click the link below to download it now!

Click here to get it FREE!!

http://bit.ly/free101recipes

© Copyright 2014 - All rights reserved.

This document is geared towards providing exact and reliable information in regards to the topic and issue covered. The publication is sold with the idea that the publisher is not required to render accounting, officially permitted, or otherwise, qualified services. If advice is necessary, legal or professional, a practiced individual in the profession should be ordered.

- From a Declaration of Principles which was accepted and approved equally by a Committee of the American Bar Association and a Committee of Publishers and Associations.

In no way is it legal to reproduce, duplicate, or transmit any part of this document in either electronic means or in printed format. Recording of this publication is strictly prohibited and any storage of this document is not allowed unless with written permission from the publisher. All rights reserved.

The information provided herein is stated to be truthful and consistent, in that any liability, in terms of inattention or otherwise, by any usage or abuse of any policies, processes, or directions contained within is the solitary and utter responsibility of the recipient reader. Under no circumstances will any legal responsibility or blame be held against the publisher for any reparation, damages, or monetary loss due to the information herein, either directly or indirectly.

Respective authors own all copyrights not held by the publisher.

The information herein is offered for informational purposes solely, and is universal as so. The presentation of the information is without contract or any type of guarantee assurance.

The trademarks that are used are without any consent, and the publication of the trademark is without permission or backing by the trademark owner. All trademarks and brands within this book are for clarifying purposes only and are the owned by the owners themselves, not affiliated with this document.

Printed in Great Britain
by Amazon